Being Prepared Without Being A Kook

Gia Scott

DEDICATION

To my Grandmothers, who taught me the value of being prepared.

Table of Contents

ACKNOWLEDGMENTS

This book is dedicated to the people who have made it possible, starting with Joe, Kelly & Terry Wayne who introduced me to the very idea of being prepared over 30 years ago now. Along the way, my skills have been honed and improved by many people, to which I will always be grateful for spending the time with me to allow me to learn.

About this book

This book has been written to explain to the average person the reasons behind an emergency preparation plan. Nobody wants to be labeled a "kook" or be shuffled off into the fringe lunatic section of society, and often, that is where "preppers" are placed. Instead, there are very real and tangible reasons to be prepared for emergencies, and the "end of the world" is the least among them.

Survivalists are often in that fringe lunatic section, and with each arrest of a "domestic terrorist" or discovery of some new oversized weapons cache, this public perception of a prepper becomes more widespread. With this perception of the entire field of emergency preparation, many people are fearful of advocating emergency preparation let alone participating in it.

That leaves us with the issue of how to be prepared without becoming a kook dancing happily in the fringe lunatic version of the balcony at the back of the theater. Taking a common sense approach to the entire issue of emergency preparation is undoubtedly the best solution to the problem. Everyone should have a basic level of emergency preparation, whether they live in an urban apartment or a rustic homestead in the woods. With this book, each family should be able to assess their risk factors and choose an emergency preparation plan that best suits their own circumstances, budget, and philosophy about life.

The myth of "end of the world kooks"

Mainstream media often portrays those who advocate being prepared as fanatics who are convinced that the end of the world is imminent. They are also strongly associated with anarchists, domestic terrorists, weapons fanatics, and all sorts of extremist advocates. But…is that really the case?

The reality is that most people who advocate the concepts of being prepared are very normal people with very normal lives. What separates them from the rest of society does not show most of the time, and is only apparent when adversity strikes.

There is the key. *Preppers*, as they are often called, are not preparing for the end of the world or for the violent overthrowing of the government. What they are prepared for is adversity, whether it is job loss, chronic health problems, financial challenges, natural disasters, epidemics, or whatever else happens.

What is being prepared?

Being prepared is not a simple case of stocking up on food, weapons, and ammunition. It's not a simple recipe of obtaining a list of items and storing them in a closet in your house either. It requires thought, effort, training, education and practicing the skills sought. Devout advocates of emergency preparation often will state that true preparedness is a lifestyle.

Preparation starts with sitting down and using your imagination. No, this is not to imagine the "end of the world", but rather to imagine various kinds of problems that are potential risks. Here is a list to start the thought process.

*__Natural disasters__ such as tornadoes, earthquakes, hurricanes, tsunamis, floods, fires, volcanic fall out, drought, blizzards, and storms.
*__Man-made disasters__ such as nuclear fallout from nuclear plant malfunction, civic unrest, strikes, martial law, war, and chemical disasters.
*__Health related disasters__ such as epidemics, disease, incapacitation, and injury.
*__Financial disasters__ such as job loss, unexpected expenses, or personal financial losses.

When you are prepared, you are capable of meeting adversity of all kinds. That is what being prepared is all about. More than a filled closet, it's a brain that is prepared to deal with the situation at hand and find a solution. After all, where would you be if the closet was destroyed or the disaster struck when you were not in your home?

Learning survival skills is great, but most important to that survival skill set is something that is not taught in a classroom or on a survival course. It is the ability to think through problems, adapt to new situations and find solutions, even when under stress in an emergency. These are intangible life skills that anyone can use in a variety of situations besides emergency survival situations, and are usually learned beginning in childhood. These are skills that are common among survivors in any dire emergency.

While these skills cannot be taught in a class, what can be learned is confidence in your use of emergency equipment and supplies, a confidence level which only occurs after long familiarity with these skills. Practice makes perfect just as readily in these skill sets as it would in playing the piano. For many people, these skill sets can be fine-tuned by camping, as it often involves using the same skills as would be required during an emergency that thrust a family out of their home. (Removal from the home, temporary shelter, alternative cooking, staying warm/cool & dry, getting along with each other, dealing with inconveniences, etc.) Monthly at-home drills can also be conducted, creating an unplugged family night tradition to practice the skills while sharing quality family time can also be integrated into your schedule.

Why bother being prepared?

The reasons to be prepared are many fold. It starts with self-preservation, but it goes further than that. Often, during disasters, emergency personnel are put at risk to save those who are at risk. Being prepared can mean that you are not only able to take care of yourself, but will be able to help others rather than needing other people's help during a variety of emergency situations.

Being prepared can mean the difference between survival and having a future for your family.

Being prepared means you have the ability to be more confident in the face of adversity as well, increasing your ability to find solutions during difficult situations. This confidence can also increase your ability to face risk taking situations. It delivers the same confidence to the entire family, better preparing them to face the reality of adversity in the future, whether it is a period of loss of income, health issues, natural disasters, or simply a financial disaster.

In addition to these types of adversity, emergency food storage can also be a hedge against inflation, because as prices rise at the grocery store, the food you are consuming was purchased at a lower price than it is currently being sold. How much have you seen prices rise in the last year on particular items on your grocery list? Food is no longer included on the federal price index, and is not taken into account when calculating the federal cost of living or assessing inflation, so these government reports no longer accurately gauge the increased costs a family typically faces.

Today, the average urban area only can feed its population for about 24-72 hours before the food supply runs out, assuming that new supplies cannot be delivered. Even that is assuming that supplies will be evenly distributed among all of its citizens. How likely is that even distribution in practice, however?

Scenarios that result in food supplies not being delivered can be easily imagined, and can range from a union strike to quarantines over disease, as well as natural disasters, terrorist attacks, and a long list of other "what-ifs". In all of these situations, being prepared can mean the difference in being very hungry and being comfortable. This situation is probably among the most likely of emergency situations induced by the behavior of mankind.

What kinds of situations should people prepare for?

The "End of the World" is not the situation to be prepared for. If the world is truly ending, it won't matter how many guns, rounds of ammunition, cases of food, or how much survival gear you possess because there won't be a world to use it on. Unless you are equipped with a spaceship capable of traveling the galaxy, you'll meet your end along with that of our world. That means that worrying about the end of the world is rather pointless.

Most disasters that strike anyone are far more personal in nature than national in nature. That's where any good advocate of emergency preparation would advise the novice to start. Few people have more than a single month's worth of cash on hand, and most people have only enough food in their house to live on for a week or two at best.

How would you cope if suddenly you had no income?

What would you do?

Other people may be faced with sudden and unexpected need to evacuate their home and the ultimate loss of their home. If fire, flood, or a severe storm was approaching your home, how would you evacuate if you had a half hour or less to depart? How would you cope if it was all suddenly gone?

Sometimes, a family is faced with a devastating illness of some sort, whether it is terminal in nature or financially devastating as treatment is sought. Increased expenses accompany those situations, as well as consumption of time of the family breadwinners as they cope with the ill family member, if it is not the breadwinner his or herself that is ill or injured. Sometimes, even if there is insurance to assist, payment is delayed or refused, making the financial disaster much more critical from the outset.

How would your family cope?

Each family's situation is unique. Their needs are equally unique. Only by imagining situations of this nature can they figure out how to prepare to meet whatever happens to occur in the future. Relying on the good will of family and friends is a precarious coping mechanism. Relying on government assistance can be even more precarious and subject to the whims of the current political climate. Even when assistance is sent to an area after a natural disaster, it is often not delivered quickly where it is needed the most, a problem that has been illustrated repeatedly in situations such as with hurricanes Katrina and Sandy.

What is essential?

There are very few truly essential items for the survival of a human being. So what are they?

Water—this is critical. We must have clean, uncontaminated water to drink. We cannot survive long without it, and in extreme temperatures, our water needs are increased.

Shelter—we need protection from the elements. How much shelter is required varies according to the climate, season, and even somewhat between people. The very young and the very old have a narrower zone of minimal comfort than the group between these extremes. It can be as simple as shade from the sun, or it can be protection from wind, cold and snow. Generally, something to keep the sun and precipitation off of the people along with protecting them from wind and wind driven precipitation is the minimal requirement.

Food—we all need to eat, and usually food provides far more than minimal energy for immediate survival, as it also provides a sense of well-being and comfort too. While fueling our bodies is critical, the comfort and well-being are also important during survival situations, especially for children. This security helps those under stress manage to retain good decision making skills and maintain a positive outlook in their overview of the situation.

Clothing—unlike animals, we are hairless and incapable of being comfortable without clothing, whether it is to protect us from sun or cold. Having clean, dry clothing to put on is important to maintaining physical and mental well-being. It is essential to have at least one full change of clothing, and having additional socks as well as sleeping garments is a good idea. Infants and young children may need more clothing than adults, especially during adverse weather conditions.

Medicine—for many people, good health means having their essential medications to treat a variety of health problems. Medication to treat minor ailments such as strained muscles, headaches, minor illnesses, etc. are also important. During emergencies, running to the local drug store may not be an option.

Security—this is preventing anyone and anything from posing a threat to you or your family's immediate survival, whether it is looters looking for an opportunity to take your supplies away or marauding packs of newly feral/abandoned dogs. Tactics for this can be as varied as simply being invisible to potential threats, clubs to chase off dogs, slingshots to chase off animals, or firearms to use as a last resort. This is a very individual choice, determined by the level of training one has or desires to obtain.

Communication—this is how you can signal to emergency personnel indicating your location or to your family members to indicate where you are. Many emergency kits include a loud, shrill whistle and mirror to use. Other alternatives can be small portable radios (walkie-talkies) or CB radios.

Entertainment—this may sound silly, but during long periods of time during an emergency, time begins to crawl as you wait for something to happen, whether it is in your home or in an emergency camp. Finding something to help occupy your time will go a long ways towards maintaining your sanity. Most emergency preparation advocates will advise people to add a paperback and a deck of cards to their emergency backpack for just this reason. Alternative card games such as Uno, Phase 10, etc. are also good alternate card decks to include, as well as dice to play games such as Yahtzee. All of these are compact & lightweight to add to an emergency backpack.

How to be prepared

Being prepared is not a simple recipe or shopping list. It is also multi-faceted, requiring at least some effort on the part of the people doing the preparation. The most critical part of being prepared is not the purchase of supplies, but rather the practicing of skills that may be needed during an emergency, whether it is construction of emergency shelters, food preparation, or first aid.

Mental Preparation

Mental preparation involves learning the skills that you and your family would need during an emergency situation. Knowing how to use survival equipment, first aid knowledge, and having an evacuation plan are all critical first steps in being mentally prepared. Having practice drills on coping with emergencies such as extended power outages, construction of an emergency shelter, staying in a tent, etc. are all important parts of that mental preparation.

Emergency Backpack

The emergency backpack is your evacuation plan and quick exit basic bag. This isn't something that is elaborate but it does contain the basics of food, shelter, clothing, food preparation tools, and first aid. Complete kits are sold, and there are many suppliers of items to use, ranging from the inexpensive to the very expensive. Your emergency backpacks should contain the essentials to survive for three days and always include a minimum of a three day supply of food and water, simple shelter, and a full change of clothing.

First Aid Kit

This is often a pre-packed kit purchased from a store, but it should be modified to include items needed by your family such as prescription medicine, regularly used OTC medications, etc. Don't forget minor wound items such as adhesive bandages, gauze, tape, hydrogen peroxide, tweezers, and steri-tape. While your emergency backpack will include a mini-first aid kit, this is a more elaborate version, and should be packed in its own container.

Bug Out Bag

While many people confuse the emergency backpack and the bug out bag (BOB) they are actually used in very different ways. The BOB is your second line evacuation supply, the bag you bring IF you have time, IF you have the room, IF you can carry it. It typically contains more food, more elaborate shelter, additional clothing, ammunition, etc.

Emergency Pantry

This is your short term emergency food supply. Typically, it will contain 3-7 days' supply of food for the entire family. This should also be easy to prepare foods requiring minimal cooking, if any. This pantry supply should also be easy to pack and compact, although its primary purpose is for use at home. This initial food supply is often packed and stored in a five gallon bucket for convenience.

Emergency Food Storage

This is the bulk department for your pantry. Focusing on long term storage and staple items, most preparation advocates suggest at least a twelve month supply of food kept on hand. Because of the size and expensive involved, this is the final step in being truly prepared. It also requires regular rotation to ensure that the food is fresh and good quality, which means it has to be food that the family is willing and able to eat in their regular diet. Familiarity with the foods stored also ensures that the food stored is food that your family is willing to eat and is familiar with the preparation methods needed to make it palatable.

Long term storage foods are packaged differently, and typically are sold in #10 cans that hold about a gallon of product. Freeze dried and dehydrated foods are commonly available, along with just-add-water dishes. Full year supply units are also sold and may fit into your long term storage food plan.

Grocery store foods are also used as part of the food supply by most people. These foods have a shorter shelf life and require regular rotation to ensure that they remain nutrient rich and fresh. Typical shelf life will range from 3-12 months, depending on the product, how long it was warehoused before being shipped, and how long it sat on the grocery store shelf.

In planning your emergency food supply, don't forget about things such as menu fatigue. This phenomenon occurs when the diet becomes monotonous and repetitive, and can result in everything from dietary deficiencies to refusal to eat sufficient food to maintain good health. Calculating overall calories and content of such nutrients as sodium, protein, fats, and carbohydrates is also important to maintain good health. In addition, vitamin and mineral content, especially in long term supplies, is another consideration to keep in mind.

Survival Skills

Survival skills are part of the entire emergency preparation process. For many people, this idea is the most daunting, but it should not be allowed to intimidate. For most people, skills of consuming insects for food, walking barefoot across miles of terrain, and foraging for food are not necessary skills or skills that they are ever likely to need.

All humans have a need for a few basics, and these needs do not change in survival or emergency situations. Water, shelter, and food are primary concerns, and they are listed in the order of importance.

Water

Having water on hand is a good start, but in some cases, it may be necessary to filter or purify water due to contamination of your main supply. Having a good water filter designed for emergency use is a good start and there are many models with a variety of price ranges available.

Knowing how to purify water without a dedicated water filter by filtering it (coffee filters or even a t-shirt) to remove the large particulates (chunks!) is the first step. Next, chemical purification using either a prepared method or common household bleach can be used. There is also boiling of water to purify it. Using all three methods should remove most contaminants, although it will not remove chemical contamination. Some filters will remove most chemical contaminants. Knowing exactly how to use each product or item to manage your water needs is just as important as purchasing the necessary items.

Food

Your emergency pantry and emergency food storage supply are also important long before you would need to put them into play. Familiarity with the foods and how they need prepared is a good start. Knowing what you like or don't like can only occur if you sample the products and integrate them in your regular routine. During an emergency, having unpleasant or disliked foods may seem like an unimportant issue, but it can increase the stress levels of both you and your family. Being familiar with the foods and serving foods that are pleasant can increase the sensation of comfort and security, making the situation easier to manage.

As part of this process, becoming familiar with your chosen emergency cooking method is also important. Use the stove; know how to fuel and light it, as well as how to regulate the flame for maximum efficiency. Have drills at least once a month to ensure the stove is in working order and that everyone is both familiar and comfortable using it to prepare meals.

Shelter

For a variety of reasons, even when remaining at home, knowing how to construct some kind of portable shelter may be necessary. Shelter can be used to create comfort, boundaries, or protect from sun, wind and rain. Most people automatically assume that portable shelter would mean that it is a tent. Relying on a tent is fine, to a degree, especially if you are familiar with its set up. In addition, one should be familiar with the construction and use of alternative shelter, especially since most people will only be including one of these alternatives in their emergency backpack. Alternative shelters typically will use a tarp as part of their construction.

Garbage Bag

Large garbage bags, especially the industrial sized drum liners, can become emergency shelter. Choose a colored one, usually black or dark green, so that it can also serve for shade. The simplest method of using them would be over a sleeping bag or blanket to protect from rain or wind. Just be aware, they do not breathe, and condensation can cause a problem as a result of moisture from perspiration.

In addition to the simple sleeping bag cover, they can also serve as shade or be used in lieu of a tarp. Some methods will require splitting the bag and/or using duct tape to secure the bag to its frame or to each other. Practice making a shelter out of these bags—they are inexpensive to use and dispose of, if it is deemed a failed attempt. The same methods as would be used for tarps can be used for garbage bags, although the bags are obviously smaller.

These garbage bags also make good floors inside of your shelter, even if the roof and walls are formed from tarps. Floors can protect your bed from moisture, as well as help keep you and your bed cleaner. They can also be filled with dry leaves, dry grass, or pine straw to create a crude sleeping pad and provide insulation from the cold ground.

Tarps

Tarps make good shelters, and some campers are advocates of using tarps rather than tents because of their versatile nature. They are also compact, lightweight, and inexpensive. There are entire websites and books devoted to tarp shelters, but the basic methods involve using ropes between trees or other supports, to which the tarp is attached or hung over. Lean-tos, A-frames, envelopes, and overhead are the most common methods.

Alternative shelters built from natural materials can also use a tarp as a waterproof roof or floor.

Foraging/Hunting

This is not a skill set that most people will ever employ. That does not mean you shouldn't bother learning how to do these things, but rather that devoting extensive amounts of time and effort are not necessarily a good investment. Learning some of these skills can increase your familiarity, comfort and confidence in the natural world. That familiarity and confidence can be invaluable, and increased comfort can also be an important facet to your overall survival success.

Defense

Firearms

Not everyone is going to include firearms in their emergency supplies, but many do think that it is a good idea. Just like any other specialized item included in your gear, learning how to use and maintain the item is important. Attend a gun safety course, ensure you have the appropriate permits/licenses to own the weapon, and store it securely. If you include a firearm of any kind in your emergency kit, don't forget to include ammunition, as without it, the firearm becomes just a bulky piece of metal of no particular use.

Alternative Defensive Tools

There are numerous defensive tools available to the general public, ranging from electronic products to simple clubs. Whether or not these items are included is an individual choice, but knowing how to use them is a critical point. No matter how expensive, simple, or useful a defense can be, if you don't know how to use it appropriately, it will not do you any good. Attending a self-defense class may also be a good choice.

Knowing why you are choosing to be prepared
Now you have the basics of what being prepared is really about. It's not about weapons caches, food hoarding, or ideology, but rather about thinking about potential problems in your future. It isn't being a kook or joining the lunatic fringe. It is merely a type of insurance for your own future.

Just like when you purchase insurance, being prepared has its own set of expenses. Just like any insurance, you can determine how much "coverage" you want and need, as well as spreading the "payment" out to suit your budget.

Emergency Preparedness Plan

Everyone should be prepared for emergencies and have an emergency preparedness plan. First, decide the amount of your resources that you can devote to your project to help you set your preparedness goals.

Most people have a set of three to five plans. These plans should dovetail together to create a comprehensive emergency preparedness plan.

Basic Plan

This is also known as the 72 hour plan and is a minimal level of preparedness. Essentially, this would include what would be necessary for the first 72 hours after an emergency. Every family should have a 72 hour plan, as this is often the minimal amount of time before emergency relief agencies can start providing services of any kind.

30 Day Plan

This includes having a 72 hour plan, and expands it to include enough food and other supplies to last for a full month. These supplies would include stored water, stored food, and personal hygiene items. This is a very good interim goal, and having a full month of supplies on hand ensures that the more minor problems such as unexpected bills, do not unduly stress your family. It should include everything your family would need to stay healthy and reasonably comfortable during the month.

90 Day Plan

This includes both the basic plan as well as supplies for three months. These supplies would include water purification, stored water, stored food, and personal hygiene items. This is a good plan for most people, as it provides them with a 90 day (3 month) safety net in case of disaster. Just like the 30 Day Plan, this plan should include all of your family's needs for the entire 90 days.

180 Day (6 Month) Plan

This is a more extensive plan, as it includes everything from the basic plan, plus enough supplies to last the entire family for six months. Like the 90 day plan, it includes water purification, stored water, stored food, and personal hygiene items. Essentially, it is everything that your family would need to stay healthy and comfortable for the entire six months without a trip to the store to purchase additional supplies. Obviously, with a bigger supply, it is a bigger safety net in case of a family facing disaster.

One Year Plan

This is the ultimate safety net with a full year of supplies in addition to that 72 hour kit. Imagine having everything on hand to completely eliminate the need to go to the store for a full year! With that full year to recover from a disaster, it definitely is a much better cushion for any family, no matter what kind of disaster they may face in the future. Larger plans, such as this one, also provide cushioning against inflation, since the food was purchased at lower cost and stored.

Getting Started

Every journey starts with a single step, and that is the same as the emergency preparation plan. So how do you get started with the plan you have chosen?

Your first step

No matter what level of preparation you have chosen to ultimately strive towards, your first step will be to acquire and set up your emergency backpacks. Each person should have their own backpack, appropriately sized so that they can comfortably carry the pack for at least an hour.

Why a backpack? Designed to be carried on your back, using shoulder straps and possibly a hip belt to support it, it leaves the user with their hands free, whether for balance, to carry additional items, or to complete some kind of task. There is less fatigue carrying a backpack as opposed to a more traditional suitcase as well.

Rotation

So what does rotation mean?

Rotation means using and replacing items on a regular and scheduled basis. This is especially important for grocery store items with their comparatively short shelf life of 90-360 days.

How do you plan on rotation?

There are several methods to rotate foods. The most common is to put newly purchased items on the back of the shelf or pantry, with older items in front. Others prefer to put the purchase date on the can to help them ensure that the item is used in appropriate order.

Long term storage foods do not require as frequent rotation with their longer shelf life. However, despite their 5-15 year shelf life, rotating items and replacing them ensures that these foods are being consumed by the family and that they are familiar with the taste, texture, appearance, and preparation required before serving.

For most efficient rotation, purchase the new item to replace the item being used, and then shift the item to be used to an entirely different area. This might be a different shelf or an entirely different storage space, depending on your particular situation. This ensures that your emergency food supply is always completely stocked, since adversity has a knack of being completely unexpected.

Basic Preparedness

There are three things that everyone should have for their emergency preparedness plan. That is the emergency medicine cabinet, emergency backpack and their emergency pantry. So what kinds of things should these three items include?

Emergency Medicine Cabinet

Your emergency medicine cabinet is different than the first aid kit. This is the supplies that you should have on hand at home, not necessarily in a truly grab-and-go portable kit. To truly understand what you should have on hand, imagine the kinds of things you may need if you could not go and purchase them for an extended period of time, as in a month.

A month may seem like a long time, impossibly long, but after many disasters, it may be a month before you are able to find an open store or are willing to stand in long lines to purchase something. In some situations, you simply may not be able to travel far enough to get to a store, whether it is because of a vehicle breakdown or a quarantine due to an epidemic or blocked roadways.

No one besides your own experience can truly dictate what should be in your medicine cabinet because of each family's unique characteristics. The list below is nothing more than suggestions, and is far from set in stone.

1 bar antibacterial soap
1# Epsom salts
1 hand & body lotion
1 shampoo
1 toothpaste
4 toothbrushes
1 mouthwash
1 oral painkiller (i.e. Orajel)
1 lg. bottle ibuprofen
1 lg. bottle aspirin

1 lg. bottle acetaminophen
1 bottle naproxen sodium
1 general vitamin/mineral supplement
1 anti-diarrheal remedy
1 stool softener
1 lg. antacid
1 loratadine
1 generic Benadryl
1 cold remedy
1 cough syrup
1 menthol rub
1 muscle rub
1 insect repellent
1 first aid spray
1 hydrocortisone cream
1 body powder
1 foot powder
1 athlete's foot remedy
1 pkg. band aids
1 gauze
1 medical tape
1 elastic bandage
 1 hydrogen peroxide
1 rubbing alcohol
1 tweezers
1 scissors
1 nail clipper
30 day supply prescription medication

Remember, many of these items also need to be rotated. The easiest method is to purchase a new item, removing the old one from the emergency medicine cabinet and move it to the stock being currently used, as these items should be the same ones that are being used in your home every day. One method of ensuring that your supplies stay together and organized is to use a tool box or plastic tote to hold these supplies separately from the ones currently in use. They can be then stored in a cool, dry closet or cupboard.

Emergency backpack

The emergency backpack should reflect the area and climate you live in, as well as the season. The backpack is your grab-and-go bag for emergency evacuations. This means that most people will need to go through their pack twice each year, replacing clothing and some of their supplies to remain appropriate for the season. Remember the purpose of the bag: it should contain everything you need to be comfortable for 3 days, from sleeping to eating. So what kinds of things would they be?

Adult Backpack

3 days of clothing, from underwear to outer clothing
Blanket (micro fleece throws are warm, compact & light)
Flat Sheet (great for many uses)
Sharp knife such as pocket knife
Multi-tool (inexpensive is fine) useful for many tasks
Cup, bowl, plate, eating utensils (everyone eats)
Personal hygiene kit (soap, washcloth, small towel, shampoo, comb, toothbrush, toothpaste, deodorant, hand sanitizer)

Sanitary supplies (tampons/napkins)
Toilet paper, 1 roll
2 drum liners, folded into zip lock bags
Compact stove (i.e. backpacker stove) & fuel
Flashlight & batteries
Paperback novel
Deck of cards
Tablet & pencil
Candle & matches
Lighter
Mess kit (for cooking)
Can opener
3 freeze dried entrees
3 freeze dried desserts
1 can fruit
1 can beans
3 pkgs. Trail mix or dried fruit
6 granola/energy bars
3 pkgs. Ramen noodles
12 hard candies
3 single serving pkts. instant coffee, tea, or other drink mix
6 bottles water

Pack these items into your backpack and add copies of important papers, photos, etc. on a small USB external drive in a small dry bag for protection from the elements. Twice a year, in spring and fall, exchange the previous season's clothing for current season's version.

Child Backpack

Children have slightly different needs than adults, and also don't need to duplicate everything an adult is carrying. In addition, they cannot carry as heavy or bulky a backpack. One advantage to children is that their clothing is smaller & lighter, increasing in bulk as the child develops and becomes stronger.

3 changes of clothing
Jacket
Rain poncho
2 small blankets
Flat sheet
Mess kit (cup, bowl, spoon, fork)
Hygiene kit (toothbrush, toothpaste, hand sanitizer, soap, shampoo, washcloth, sm. Towel)
2 drum liners, folded into zip lock bags
Flashlight & batteries
Can opener
24 hard candies (individually wrapped)
3 freeze dried entrees
6 granola/energy bars
3 pkgs. Dried fruit
3 pkgs. Nuts or nut butter
3 pkgs. Dried fruit
3 pkgs. Instant cereal
3 pkgs. Cookies
3 cans Vienna sausages
3 pkgs. Crackers
3-6 bottles of water (depending on child)
1 stuffed toy/doll (comfort item)
1 small action figure
1 small favorite story book

Infant Backpack

Obviously, infants cannot carry their own backpack. They need carried, if the family is moving on foot, as well as their essentials. To carry the infant, a front load carrier is a good investment to prevent discomfort to both mother and child, since most infants will want their mothers to carry them at least a good portion of the time. To better divide the load, the infant's essentials should be packed into a separate bag to allow it to be moved to the non-infant carrying adult. This can be a duffle bag, along with 2 or 3 compression straps to allow it to be strapped to a backpack quickly & easily.

24 disposable diapers
1 pkg. wipes
1 can powdered formula
1 box instant rice cereal
9 jars of baby food
Spoon
3 bottles w/nipples
3 bottles juice
9 bottles water
9 pkgs. Pediatric electrolyte beverage mix
9 teething biscuits (older infants)
6 prs. Socks
3 footed sleepers
1 blanket sleeper
1 knit hat
3 pants
3 onesies
3 t-shirts
2 long sleeved shirts
1 bib

3 light blankets
3 fleece blankets
1 flat sheet

Emergency Pantry

In your emergency pantry, plan for fast preparation with minimal heating or effort. Prepared canned items, mixes, and freeze dried (just add water) items work great. The amounts and particular items can vary between families. This is also for grab-and-go purposes, and should be stored in a container that makes them quickly portable, such as a duffle bag, tote, or toolbox.

It needs to include 3 breakfasts, 3 lunches, and 3 dinners in addition to 6 snack items per person. While freeze dried items are easy to prepare, they are also much more expensive. While this is something that can and should be individualized for each family, here is a sample list of what an emergency pantry would contain for a family of four.

1 container instant dry milk
1 box complete (just add water) pancake mix
1 bottle pancake syrup
1# quick oatmeal
1# raisins
1 box tea bags
1 small jar instant coffee
1 container hot cocoa mix
1 container presweetened fruit flavored drink
1 small container nondairy creamer
1# sugar
1 pkg. cookies
1 pkg. crackers
1 jar cheese spread
1 jar peanut butter
1# spaghetti pasta
1# egg noodles
1 large box instant rice

2 pkgs. Country gravy mix
2 pkgs. Mushroom gravy mix
2 pkgs. Brown gravy mix
1 pkg. taco seasoning
1 container cinnamon
1 container pepper
1 container salt
1 jar hot sauce
2 cans chicken
1 can roast beef in gravy
1 can tuna
1 large can refried beans
1 can mushrooms
1 can Chinese vegetables
1 can peas & carrots
1 can peas
1 can corn
1 can spaghetti sauce w/meat
5 gallons water
1 camping stove w/fuel (propane, butane, white gas, etc.)

So what would this list make?

Breakfast:
#1 oatmeal with cinnamon, raisins & milk, along with cocoa, coffee or tea
#2 pancakes with syrup, cocoa, coffee or tea
#3 oatmeal with cinnamon, raisins, & milk, along with coffee, tea or cocoa

Lunch:
#1 Rice & country gravy w/chicken & peas, along with

fruit flavored drink

#2 Rice with taco seasoning & corn, refried beans, & fruit flavored drink

#3 Rice with brown gravy & Chinese vegetables, coffee, tea or cocoa

Dinner:

#1 Pasta with spaghetti sauce, coffee, tea or cocoa

#2 Noodles with country gravy w/chicken & peas & carrots, coffee, tea, or cocoa

#3 Rice with mushroom gravy, roast beef, Chinese vegetables & mushrooms, coffee, tea, cocoa

Snacks:

#1 cookies

#2 cookies & hot beverage

#3 raisins

#4 crackers with cheese spread

#5 crackers with peanut butter

#6 crackers with peanut butter & hot beverage

The important consideration is that everything for all of these meals is shelf-stable goods, and in this case they are all grocery store offerings found in almost any grocery store. These items are your first line of defense against adversity and also need regular rotation, at least every six months and best would be every three months.

Long Term Preparedness

Once you have established your basic 72 hour supplies, it's time to move on towards your next goal, the 30 day supply.

30 Day Supply

This is still a type of preparation that doesn't require shopping for long term storage foods in #10 cans, but it does mean a bit more bulk. It also doesn't exclusively feature just quick cooking foods. This focuses on just plain everyday food, including beans, pasta, rice, and flour. While this list may not work for your family, it can be a starting point to creating your own menus, shopping list, and pantry inventory. It's also a good way to start being more conscious of the food you eat, as well as encouraging you to try your hand at food preservation at home.

10# long grain brown rice
2# pinto beans
2# kidney beans
2# great northern beans
1# lentils
1# black-eyed peas
1# split peas
2# lima beans
5# assorted pasta
15# all-purpose flour
5# whole wheat flour
5# cornmeal
2# oatmeal
1# farina

2# complete pancake mix
10# sugar
4# brown sugar
2# powdered sugar
2 Lg. box/can instant dry milk
2 cans instant egg whites
1 can whole dehydrated egg powder
1# baking soda
1 baking powder
Cinnamon
Nutmeg
Allspice
Ginger
Garlic powder
Onion powder
Celery salt
Cumin
Chili powder
Oregano
Basil
Rosemary
Thyme
Caraway
Anise seed
Bay leaf
Black pepper
1# iodized salt
1# sea salt
1# active dry yeast
Vanilla
Maple flavor
Lemon flavor
1 qt. honey

1 qt. molasses
1 qt. cider vinegar
2 bottles pancake syrup
24 cans tomatoes
12 cans green beans
12 cans carrots
12 cans peas
12 cans corn
12 cans creamed corn
12 cans collards
12 cans kale
12 cans beets
4 boxes crackers
4 pkg. cookies
12 cans chicken
12 cans tuna
4 cans meat (Spam, etc.)
2 cans mackerel
2 qts. Vegetable oil
2 cans shortening
4 beef stew
6 spaghetti sauce with meat
1 can parmesan cheese
2 boxes processed cheese spread
4 cans mushrooms
6 jars assorted jellies & jams
12 cans peaches
12 cans pineapple
4 cans mandarin oranges
4 cans cherry pie filling
4 cans blueberry pie filling
2 jars applesauce
3 large cans coffee

1 lg. tea bags
2 lg. cocoa mix
4 canisters assorted fruit flavored drink mix
2# raisins
1# dried cherries
2# dried cranberries
2# prunes
2# dried apples
2# beef jerky
1 standard first aid kit
1 pkg. adhesive bandages
1 acetaminophen (100 caplets)
1 ibuprofen (100 tablets)
1 aspirin (100 tablets)
1 Benadryl or generic (50 caplets)
1 general vitamin supplement (100 ct.)
1 loratadine (50 ct.)
1 box cold remedy (24 ct.)
1 menthol rub
1 muscle rub
1 hydrocortisone cream
1 rubbing alcohol
1 hydrogen peroxide
1 insect repellent
1 pkg. aluminum foil
1 pkg. plastic wrap
1 pkg. gallon zip lock bags (25 ct.)
1 pkg. quart zip lock bags (25 ct.)
1 pkg. plastic storage bags w/twist ties (25 ct.)
1 pkg. tall kitchen trash bags (25 ct.)
50' clothesline rope
Clothespins (50 ct.)
Duct tape

Super glue
1 dish soap
1 qt. bleach
1 gallon distilled vinegar
1 toothpaste
1 mouthwash
1 bar soap
1 shampoo
1 sunscreen
1 hand & body lotion
1 small bottle liquid laundry detergent
5 gallon bucket
16 rolls toilet paper
4 rolls paper towels
2 boxes facial tissues
Fuel for camp stove (propane, butane, or white gas) for a full month

This makes a long list, and while the quantities and particular foods included may not be the same as your family would use, it does give you an idea of what should be on that 30-day inventory list. For best results, try actually using only what you have on the inventory for a week to ensure that the household cook has reasonably estimated what can and will be used to prepare meals. If it isn't something that you would normally be willing to eat, you are probably are not going to want to eat it during an emergency situation either.

In addition to food, there are other items such as aluminum foil, plastic wrap, and bags. These items are to aid in storing, cooking, and protecting foods. There is also a number of OTC (over the counter) medications listed. These medications may vary between families and are merely a representation of what your family would want to include. Remember, if it is a true emergency situation, there may not be any drug store, doctor or dentist available.

3 Month (90 day) Supply

Logic says that simply multiplying what you have in your 30 day supply would make for a three month supply. While it can be that simple, that may not be the best choice you can make. There are some new issues that need to be considered starting at the 90 day mark.

One of these issues is quality. While grocery store foods are sold to us in good quality (or should be!) that doesn't mean that sitting on our pantry shelf they will stay in good quality for 90 days or longer. Certain problems are apt to appear.

Some of these problems are specific to dry goods such as beans, rice, flours, pastas, meals, and similar items. Both insects and rodents can launch attacks against these products that will ruin them, leaving you with useless product containers on a soiled shelf. To package these items so that insects and rodents cannot attack them is nearly impossible, leaving you looking for alternative solutions.

That's where the long term storage foods come into the picture. These items are packaged in airtight containers to preserve their quality. This also makes them more impervious to both rodents and insects with minimal additional effort, ensuring that their quality is as good when you open the container as it was when the container was sealed. While it is not necessary to purchase all long term storage foods for the 90 day supply, it is advisable to start purchasing some of these items at this point. These freeze dried, dehydrated, or simply airtight packaged products may seem to be expensive, but they also will add variety to your menus, as long as you experiment with using the products before committing to large quantities of them. Many companies sell a sample size or small size can (#2 ½ can) for this reason. For smaller families, these smaller cans may be preferred for many products as the product of choice as well.

Variety is also the best prevention for another problem common with long term storage food plans: menu fatigue. So what is menu fatigue? It means that you get sick and tired of eating the same thing over and over. While it may be nutritionally sound food, most people prefer some variety in their meals. Without that variety, they may become more depressed, agitated, and prone to emotional outbursts that have nothing directly to do with the food itself.

Variety also increases the likelihood of a complete diet and reduces the likelihood of nutritional deficiencies. Humans are designed to have a varied diet, and our ancestors ate whatever was in season along with whatever they could preserve by drying, smoking, pickling or fermenting. While they often suffered from nutritional deficiencies, especially in adverse conditions, the whole point of being prepared is to avoid such situations.

Planning ahead means planning for menu variations and a variety of foods as well.

Just imagine eating beans with cornbread or rice every single day, all three meals. While you would not starve to death, you may start suffering from nutritional deficiencies and you would certainly not be pleased at seeing the same meal over and over for months on end. At the same time, if the variation is something that tastes so horrible to you that you cannot bear to eat it, it won't do anyone any good. For that reason, anything that is truly unfamiliar to you in the kitchen or at the table is worth purchasing a small amount for experimentation.

In my case, the mystery has been textured vegetable protein. I experimented with chicken flavored, thinking it would be inoffensive and easy to use. Unfortunately, I bought a #10 can to work with, and never did find any method of preparation that worked for us. The texture was like wet cardboard if it was cooked very long at all, and if it wasn't cooked, it was reminiscent of the artificial bacon bits at a salad bar: crunchy, sweet, and a bit salty. Mixed with other foods, the sweet flavor came through strongly, with an overwhelming fake flavor that was far from pleasant. I never did find a way to "hide" the stuff in something that we could eat with anything resembling pleasure. Usually, it was either refused after the first bite or soon after, and I was lucky if the sampling victim didn't actually gag. Reviewers of the various flavors on the company websites did not seem to have the same problem or else they were more accustomed to the flavor of TVP. I know that we have consumed a great deal of TVP in processed foods, but I'm not sure how they hid it—I never found a home method that worked. For that reason, we do not include any TVP in our food storage plan.

There are a variety of products available besides the TVP that we disliked. Meats, cheeses, and even things like sour cream powder are all available. Many of the companies offer a cookbook for sale using these mysterious items, and others have recipes available free from their customers on their website too. Most of the products are easy to use without special recipes, such as the fruits, vegetables and meats, as all they need is rehydration and cooking.

In addition to products such as these, they offer staples in shelf stable, rodent resistant and insect-proof #10 cans such as rice, flour, salt, sugar, pastas, etc. There are also a variety of freeze dried meals that are packaged in these #10 cans that simply need boiling water and minimal cooking to have them ready to eat.

In addition to these items, there are MREs (Meals Ready to Eat) that are similar to those packaged for military usage. These can be bought either packaged as complete meals or individually. These can be reheated by immersion in boiling water or with the chemically activated packets that are often included with the complete meals. They are quick, easy, and most are very tasty. They are also very portable, and many people like to include a small number of these with their overall food storage plan because of these characteristics. However, they are somewhat bulky and heavy to carry in any quantity.

Here's a sample list for a 90 Day Supply. These items would be in addition to those found on the 30 Day Supply lists.

Grocery Store Items

20# all-purpose flour
10# whole wheat flour
40# sugar
10# brown sugar
8# powdered sugar
6 large cans instant dry milk
5 large nondairy creamers
12 lg. cans coffee
4 lg. instant coffees
5 large canisters hot cocoa mix
2 unsweetened cocoa
6 lg. vegetable oil
3 shortening
10# cornmeal
10# oatmeal
3# farina
10# assorted pasta
5# pinto beans
5# great northern white beans
5# navy beans
5# kidney beans
3# lentils
3# split peas
3# lima beans
15# long grain white rice
5 baking powder
6 baking soda
6# salt
2# kosher salt

2# cornstarch
5 pancake syrups
1 gallon cider vinegar
3 gallons distilled vinegar
2 quarts molasses
4# active dry yeast
5# raisins
5# prunes
6 boxes crackers
12 pkgs. cookies
24 cans tuna
24 cans chicken
24 cans mackerel
6 cans Spam
12 cans corn
12 cans peas
12 cans green beans
12 cans spinach
12 cans evaporated milk
12 sm. Jars peanut butter
12 sm. honey
12 cans spaghetti sauce
12 cans peaches
12 cans pineapple
12 cans pears
12 cans fruit cocktail
6 applesauce
6 cans mandarin oranges
6 cans cherry pie filling
6 cans blueberry pie filling
5 aluminum foil
4 plastic wrap
6 pkg. gallon zip lock bags

6 pkg. quart zip lock bags
2 pkg. sandwich zip lock bags
2 pkg. gallon plastic bags (twist tie closure)
5 dish soap
6 bars soap
6 shampoo
6 deodorants
6 toothpastes
5 gallons bleach
12 rolls paper towels
6 boxes facial tissue
96 rolls toilet paper
1 qt. ammonia
2 lg. containers liquid laundry detergent
1 pkg. drum liners
2 rolls duct tape
1 lg. gorilla glue
100' rope
2 tarps (8x10)
2 pkg. large trash bags
1 pkg. tall kitchen trash bags
6 bottles peroxide
6 bottles rubbing alcohol
5 hand & body lotions
2 sunscreens
5 insect repellents
6 hydrocortisone cream
2 cans Dermoplast (spray first aid)
4 boxes adhesive bandages
2 rolls adhesive tape
2 lg. boxes gauze pads
3 pkg. cheese cloth
6 pkg. coffee filters

5 acetaminophen (100 caplets)
5 ibuprofen (100 tablets)
5 aspirin (100 tablets)
5 Benadryl or generic (50 caplets)
5 general vitamin supplements (100 ct.)
3 calcium supplements (100 ct.)
5 loratadine (50 ct.)
3 box cold remedy (24 ct.)
3 lg. antacid tablets (calcium based)
3 anti-diarrhea pills (50 ct.)
2 laxatives (25 ct.)
2 menthol rubs
5 muscle rubs
Basic sewing kit (needles, thread, buttons)

In addition to these locally purchased items, certain long term storage items would be a good choice. Here is a sample list.

6 cans all-purpose flour
1 can whole wheat flour
2 cans white rice
1 can barley
1 can cornmeal
1 can oatmeal
2 cans sugar
2 can egg noodles
1 can elbow macaroni
1 can whole grain cereal
1 can granola
1 can muffin mix

1 can multi-grain pancake mix
1 can freeze dried ground beef
1 can freeze dried roast beef
1 can freeze dried chicken
1 can freeze dried sausage crumbles
2 cans whole eggs
2 cans shredded potatoes
2 cans cubed potatoes
1 can chopped onion
1 can freeze dried peas
1 can freeze dried green beans
1 can freeze dried carrot slices
1 can freeze dried red bell pepper dices
1 can freeze dried mushrooms
1 can freeze dried celery
1 can stew vegetables
1 can tomato powder
1 can freeze dried peaches
1 can freeze dried pears
2 cans freeze dried apples
1 can freeze dried raspberries
1 can freeze dried blueberries
1 can freeze dried applesauce
2 cans dehydrated refried beans
4 cans dry pinto beans
1 can dry kidney beans
2 cans butter powder
6 cans instant milk powder
1 can dehydrated cheese blend powder
1 can dehydrated mozzarella cheese
1 can dehydrated cheddar cheese
2 cans fruit flavored drink mix

Remember that these lists are not set in stone, as each family should make up their own list of what they would actually use and enjoy. Some families may prefer to invest in more of the long term storage foods at this point as well, largely to reduce the effort in rotating grocery store supplies. Others may prefer to add more of the just-add-water prepared meals.

6 Month Supply (180 Days)

It's at this point when multiplication begins to be useful, but at the same time, one wants diversity among their stored supplies. So what does that really mean?

It means that multiplication can be useful on the core supplies such as protein sources, dairy products, flour, sugar, rice, pasta and beans. When looking at your long term supplies however, you may wish to consider diversifying your fruits, vegetables, and beverages.

Long Term Storage foods (#10 cans)

1 Pearled Barley
2 Cracked Wheat Cereal
2 Whole grain cereal
1 creamy wheat cereal
3 Cornmeal
6 All Purpose Flour
4 Whole Wheat Flour
2 Granola
2 Egg Noodles
3 Elbow Macaroni
3 Spaghetti pasta
2 Quick Oats
1 Old Fashioned Oatmeal
1 Popcorn
4 White Rice
1 cornstarch
1 Beef Gravy Mix
1 Chicken Gravy Mix

2 honey
1 Creamy soup base
2 Brown sugar
2 Powdered Sugar
6 Granulated Sugar
1 Apple dices
1 applesauce
1 Apricot pieces
1 Triple Berry Mix
1 Blackberry
1 Whole Blueberry
1 Cherry
1 Peach Dices
1 Pineapple Dices
1 Raisins
1 Asparagus pieces
1 Green Beans
1 Broccoli
1 Cauliflower
1 Carrot Slices
1 Sweet Corn
1 Green Pepper Dices
1 Freeze dried Mushrooms
1 freeze dried Onion flakes
1 Peas
1 Potato Dices
2 Potato Flakes
2 Complete Mashed Potatoes
2 Spinach Flakes
1 Tomato Chunks
2 tomato powder
1 Butter powder
2 shredded Cheddar cheese

2 Shredded Mozzarella cheese
1 Monterey Jack cheese
2 Scrambled Egg Mix
1 Egg White
2 Whole Egg powder
6 instant Nonfat dry milk
1 Sour cream powder
2 Black bean
2 kidney bean
1 lentil
2 pinto beans
2 refried beans
2 white beans
2 split peas
2 buttermilk biscuit mix
1 muffin mix
2 blueberry muffin mix
2 brownie mix
2 whole wheat roll mix
1 apple drink mix
1 orange drink mix
1 peach drink mix
1 hot chocolate mix
1 Buttermilk pancake mix
2 blueberry pancake mix
2 apple pancake mix
2 whole grain pancake mix
1 instant chocolate pudding mix
1 instant vanilla pudding mix
1 potato soup mix
1 ground beef
2 roast beef
1 cooked white meat chicken

1 ham
1 pork patty crumbles
1 sausage crumbles
1 creamy strawberry drink mix
1 creamy chocolate drink mix
1 creamy vanilla drink mix
1 Freeze dried Vegetable Stew with Beef

Grocery Store Items

Once you start on longer term storage, it is essential to reduce your dependence on grocery store items with their shorter shelf life. At the six month mark, some items are still essential.

1 quart honey
4 32 oz. vegetable oil
2 lg. shortening
2 lg. cocoa powder
20# sugar
20# white flour
2 lg. complete pancake mix
2 lg. buttermilk baking mix
1 baking powder
2 lg. baking soda
5# salt
3 lg. maple flavored syrup
3 lg. coffee
3 lg. coffee creamer
3 lg. boxes tea bags
3 lg. hot cocoa mix
2 lg. hot apple cider mix
2 lg. instant coffee

24 jars jellies/jams
12 cans pineapple
12 cans peaches
12 cans fruit cocktail
5 cherry pie filling
5 blueberry pie filling
24 cans tuna
12 cans chicken
6 cans Spam (or similar)
4 lg. processed cheese loaves
12 boxes assorted crackers
12 cans beef stew
5# assorted pasta
10# assorted beans
10# brown rice
12 cans/jars spaghetti sauce
2 barbecue sauce
2 mustard
2 ketchup
10# brown sugar
4# powdered sugar
2 boxes mashed potatoes
1 gallon bleach
2 lg. laundry detergent
2 toothpaste
2 hand & body lotion
1 band-aids
1 gauze
1 medical tape
1 hydrogen peroxide
1 rubbing alcohol
1 first aid spray
1 hydrocortisone cream

1 lg. ibuprofen
1 lg. acetaminophen
1 lg. aspirin
1 lg. cold medicine
1 cough syrup
1 lg. loratadine
1 lg. generic Benadryl
1 anti-diarrhea remedy
1 stool softener
1 muscle rub
1 menthol rub
1 general vitamin/mineral supplement
1# Epsom salts
2 shampoo
6 bars soap
1 duct tape
1 lg. trash bag
6 rolls paper towels
92 rolls toilet paper
2 wet wipes
1 gallon zip lock bag
1 quart zip lock bag
1 sandwich zip lock bag
2 lg. dish soap
1 gallon cider vinegar
1 gallon white vinegar
2# instant yeast

12 Month Supply (365 Days)

At this point in your food storage plan, a larger portion should be devoted to long term storage foods to ensure that the food is fresh and tasty when it is needed. It's a much larger selection of food with increased variety because the goal of this supply is to render a shopping trip unnecessary for a full year.

Long Term Storage (#10 cans)

6 Multi-grain rolled cereal
6 Granola
6 Egg Noodles
6 elbow macaroni
6 spaghetti
1 popcorn
6 white rice
6 cornmeal
3 rolled oats
2 creamy wheat cereal
2 cracked wheat cereal
12 white flour
6 whole wheat flour
1 black beans
2 kidney beans
1 lentil
2 pinto beans
2 refried beans
2 navy beans
1 split pea
1 creamy broccoli soup mix
3 honey

1 Creamy soup mix

3 Brown sugar

1 powdered sugar

6 white sugar

1 apple slices

1 apricot dices

1 berry blend

1 blackberry

1 blueberry

1 cherry

1 strawberry slices

3 broccoli

3 carrot slices

1 celery

2 mixed stew vegetables

1 sliced mushrooms

1 chopped onion

3 peas

6 potato dices

1 diced sweet potato

1 shredded hash browns

2 complete mashed potatoes

3 spinach

3 tomato powder

2 zucchini

1 asparagus

2 green bean

1 butter powder

2 cheese blend powder

2 colby cheese

2 cheddar cheese

2 mozzarella cheese

1 monterey jack cheese

1 creamy banana drink
1 creamy chocolate drink
1 creamy vanilla drink
1 creamy strawberry drink
3 scrambled egg mix
1 egg white
3 whole egg powder
6 instant nonfat dry milk powder
1 ground beef
2 roast beef
3 white meat chicken
1 ham
2 sausage crumbles
2 turkey
1 orange drink mix
1 apple drink mix
1 peach drink mix

Grocery Store Items

At the 12 month mark, there are not many products that can stay fresh and wholesome for any longer. There are, however, a few items that do stay stable.

20# sugar
5# salt
3 large baking soda
1 baking powder
2 qts. Molasses
5# hard candies, individually wrapped
3 lg. maple flavored syrup

2# raisins
2# prunes
Assorted spices and flavorings
1 gallon white vinegar
2 gallons cider vinegar
1 duct tape
1 lg. trash bags
2 gallon zip lock bag
1 quart zip lock bag
1 sandwich zip lock bag
1 gallon bleach
3 lg. laundry detergent
2 lg. dish soap
2 shampoo
6 bars soap
2 toothpaste
4 toothbrushes
1 cold remedy
1 cough syrup
1 ibuprofen
1 aspirin
1 acetaminophen
1 general vitamin/mineral supplement
1 anti-diarrhea remedy
1 stool softener
6 rolls paper towels
92 rolls toilet paper
1 fiber supplement
1 hydrogen peroxide
1 rubbing alcohol
1 hydrocortisone cream
1 first aid spray
1 muscle rub

1 menthol rub
1 pkg. band-aids
5# Epsom salts
2 wet wipes
2 hand & body lotions
2 lg. sunscreens
2 lg. insect repellant

Long Term Storage Realities

There are some realities about the long term storage that need to be taken into account. It's a lot of food and supplies, and they are both heavy and bulky. They need space.

People can be very creative about finding space for their long term storage foods. I've seen cases stacked up together and covered with a table cloth to make a coffee table. I've seen bedframes supported by cases of #10 cans, and I've seen the cans stacked behind the sofa. Most people designate a closet as their storage point, but for a full year's worth, it needs to be a large closet. A giant walk-in pantry is ideal, but not all houses are equipped with one.

Some people look at their attic or garage as their storage point. This might not be the best option, as these areas are not climate controlled, and storing foods in areas that become far too hot for ideal storage. Garages are also the location for chemicals that we just don't like our foods to be exposed to, rendering them less than ideal as well as potentially too hot. Basements, in houses that include them, are another location that often introduces new problems, due to the dampness of such spaces.

Cool and dry are critical characteristics for long term storage of food's shelf life. Each home and family is unique in their needs as well as their storage assets. Anybody can store the emergency basics of medicine cabinet, first aid kit, back pack, and pantry, and almost all can accommodate the 30 Day Supply. Most, with some creativity, can also manage the 90 Day Supply without

71

serious inconvenience. 6 and 12 month supplies often require serious commitment, not only for the purchase but the storage of the additional quantities.

No matter what your circumstances are, trying to establish that 90 Day Supply should be an important and high priority goal for your family.

If you are processing food yourself for your food storage program, home canned and dehydrated goods will often require even more space. This food must also have the cool, dry, and dark area to store the food for maximum nutritional value.

Pets and Emergencies

We love our pets and usually consider them family members. If it is necessary to evacuate your home, it is always best to bring your pet along. Having your pet's own emergency pack is a great idea. While backpacks for dogs do exist, most dogs are incapable of carrying all of their own food and water for even three days in one. As an alternative, using a duffle bag is probably your best choice.

Pet Evacuation Kit

Each pet should have their own bag, and color coding them makes it easy to recognize which bag goes with which pet. Here's what each bag should include.

7 days dry food supply
7 days canned food supply
Treats
Spare leash & collar (harness for cats)
Tie out cable
Blanket (for bed)
Coat
Chew toy (for dogs)
Cat toy (for cats)
Small litter pan (for cats)
Small bag of cat litter (for cats)
Current vaccination print out from veterinarian
Photo of pet
Food & water dishes
Medication (if needed)

In addition to these items packed in a bag, have a portable crate (wire crates fold up compactly) along with a gallon of water. A crate is important because many motels and shelters will require a crate for your pet, if you are forced to evacuate to one. In addition, crates make it easier to confine your pet safely, if necessary.

Long Term Supplies

When planning your long term storage supplies, including your pet is a good idea. Kibble or dry food is your best option for long term storage, and it must be kept in a container safe from insect and rodent infestations. Five gallon buckets with tightly sealed lids are idea. There are also lids available for purchase to fit these buckets that have a screw-out center, making access much easier. Including an oxygen absorber may help in the food staying fresher longer. Use your regular pet food to fill these containers. In addition to their regular food, including treats, cat litter (for cats), and other essentials such as flea treatments is a good idea. Remember, some of the best reasons for storing supplies is as an insurance policy against price increases, supply problems, or lack of funds to purchase them.

Additional Food Supplies

All of your food does not have to arrive in a can or carton. Having additional sources will help you be prepared to meet the future by reducing your food expenditures and diversifying your food supply. Raising it or obtaining it can also increase your physical well-being by encouraging exercise and activity.

The Garden

Everybody prefers fresh food, and it is usually far healthier for us than any type of preserved food. In uncertain times, maintaining a garden is often a very good idea for any household. Food from this garden supplements the food purchased from the grocery store and can also be part of your long term storage plan by preserving these foods. Even just raising a few herbs in pots or a flower bed can be a great asset and cost saving project, as herbs are among our most expensive purchases on the grocer's shelves.

Small Livestock

Not everyone is capable of owning and caring for small livestock but for many people, it is another option to consider. Chickens, ducks, rabbits, and goats are among the most common small livestock kept. Keep in mind that these animals need daily care and clean up, and that livestock often also includes the necessity of killing and butchering these animals. Not everyone is capable of doing this, and therefore it may not be a good project for your family. In addition, there are often ordinances that prevent people from keeping livestock of any kind on their property.

If this is something you are considering, do your research. Try working with these animals to see if you are capable of managing them efficiently and humanely. There are numerous books, videos, and other material dedicated to explaining their needs and management.

If you do choose to keep these animals, eggs, meat, and milk are the primary products produced. Learning to use the milk to make cheese is a great activity when keeping goats. Having fresh eggs and meat, even when the grocery stores are closed or unavailable is also a great advantage. Just remember to store appropriate foods in sufficient quantities to feed your livestock as well. For pellets and grain, metal garbage cans, along with a bungee cord to keep the lid tightly attached, make for good rodent resistant storage.

Foraging locally

Knowing what grows in your area that is edible is also a great idea, along with knowing where various people are growing fruit trees locally. These sources can provide fruit, berries, and greens to make everything from jellies and jams to canned or dried greens long before the emergency strikes. During an emergency, these food sources may remain available, supplementing your stored food reserves.

Many homeowners with fruit or nut trees may regard them as a messy item and not have plans to use much, if any, of the fruit and nuts resulting. These homeowners may look on your request to pick or harvest these items as a great way to help with cleanup. Others may be willing to part with part of their crop in exchange for some jam or jelly made from it. Still other sources may be publicly available, at least to partial access, as they grow over fences or on right-of-ways. Explore your options!

Home food preservation

Learning how to preserve food at home can be fun. It can be pickled, fermented, dried or canned. It can make sweets to dress up a slice of bread, or fancy pickles to serve at holiday dinners. Dried fruit can be used in a variety of dishes as well. Fermented fruits and vegetables include everything from homemade wine to sauerkraut. Each process does have its own benefits, and requires its own equipment too.

Dehydration

In some areas of the country, dehydration via solar methods works well. In these areas of low humidity, something as simple as a rack in the sun with a screen to prevent insect infestation can be used to dry foods. In other areas, with higher humidity, a dehydrator is essential.

When purchasing a dehydrator, choose a model with a temperature gauge that allows you to adjust between several settings. Herbs, fruits & vegetables, and meats all require different settings. Also ensure you have a tray liner to dry more liquid things such as fruit puree or tomato puree, for greater versatility.

There are a number of books on the market that give directions on how to dehydrate foods, as well as recipes using these foods. It is recommended that the novice embarking on dehydration invests in one or more of these books.

Canning

Essentially, there are two methods of canning: hot water bath and pressure canning. The method used depends on the item being canned. High acid foods and jams/jellies are the only foods canned with the water bath method.

Canning does require some initial investments which are rather expensive. These include the water bath canner, pressure canner, jars with lids & rings, and the ingredients to process the foods. Some pickles are also made using the hot water bath canner.

Canning is another food processing method that there are a number of books on the topic available. The standard reference for decades has been the Ball Blue Book. It is sold at the usual sources online, and is available in home improvement centers, discount stores, and often even your grocery store.

Pickling

Many pickles are made and processed in a water bath canner. Other pickles are naturally fermented and require the use of a crock, often with a weighted lid to press the food down for good fermentation. These large crocks are expensive. Like the other food preservation methods, there are books that describe the process clearly, as well as giving recipes to make the products, and often to use them.

Fermentation for wine, beer, ale & cider

Making wine is an art form in itself. There are complete kits for novices available, as well as books on the topic. The same is true of beer, ale, and cider. Consulting these sources for recipes is highly recommended, as many things can go wrong with inexperienced dabblers of the art.

Freezing

For long term storage, freezing foods is somewhat frowned upon. It is not because of the poor quality of the food so much as it is the reality of life indicates that if the emergency food is needed, there may be a very high likelihood that there is no electricity to power your freezer. Without electricity, the food will thaw and then spoil. Canned, freeze dried, and dehydrated foods, whether purchased or home processed, is much less dependent on the delivery of power to stay fresh and wholesome.

Social Aspects of Emergency Preparation

While some people avoid anyone knowing about their preparedness state, others prefer a more social experience. There are some advantages to belonging to a group of preppers, such as sharing of equipment and expertise. For others, group purchases are the big appeal, as these group purchases mean that the group can get more items at a lower cost than if each person was purchasing individually.

Finding others

It's not easy to find others, as few appear on a list anywhere as a prepper. If you currently belong to a church or social organization that advocates emergency preparation, you have a built in organization with others of a like mind, as well as the potential for finding experts to increase your own knowledge. For others, establishing their own organization might provide them with the only available method of finding like-minded individuals.

As with any group of people, preppers can be variable in nature. Some have already signed up to join the lunatic fringe. Others are more moderate. Some may be fanatics about the prepping process. Not all groups will suit all preppers, nor will all preppers be someone that you will enjoy spending time with.

Related Groups

Sometimes, finding a group that suits you will mean a group other than a prepper group. Homesteading groups will often be appropriate too, as these individuals are dedicated to being self-sufficient and will use many of the same skills that you may be seeking. For outdoors skills, such as survival skills, outdoor and camping organizations might be more appropriate

About the Author

Gia Scott was born, just like everyone else, but she also was born to a family that included politicians, used car dealers, and horse traders. Along with that illustrious lineage, she was related to vaudeville performers, horse trainers, cowboys, entrepreneurs, teachers, and preachers. With such diversity surrounding her from childhood, she still managed to grow up and develop a deep love of books. It was only natural that along the way, she would write them too. The Survivors: The Time of Chaos is her first published novel. More will undoubtedly follow. Freak Files: The Unexplained Tales is a collection of stories believed to be true to life.

After decades of experimental cooking, much to her family's chagrin (after all, the family is inflicted with the less-than-wonderful versions that never see print!) Gia began writing food articles and a food blog. It was inevitable that cookbooks would follow. This is the sixth cookbook. Previous titles include: All Chocolate—Easy & Economical Recipes Anyone Can Make At Home, 55 Fantastic Fudges, The All American Biscuit, 55 Frightfully Fun Foods, and A Home Style Thanksgiving.

Today, after many incarnations along the way, Gia Scott lives in Mississippi with her husband, three dogs, and two cats in a funny little house surrounded by very big and gnarly trees. Having reached that age of privilege, she can often be found in her garden, wearing peculiar clothes and tending her plants. When she can talk her husband into it, they enjoy going for road trips, looking for the elusive town of New Hope. In between road trips and gardening, she manages to fit in an internet radio talk show called the Dawn of Shades, interviewing a variety of people, including other authors, and promoting causes dear to her heart.

In addition to all of that, she still maintains blogs on general topics, cooking & food, and camping, emergency preparedness & outdoors activities. She also helps with content for websites.

Links

Gia's other books can be found right here.

Gia's general blog is found at www.giascott.wordpress.com.

Gia's food blog is found at www.gulfcoastfoods.wordpress.com.

Gia's camping blog is found at www.getreadygo.wordpress.com.

Her website is found at www.exogenynetwork.com

Her author page on Facebook is found at www.facebook.com/giascottblogs

Gia can be emailed directly at giascott@exogenynetwork.com. She would be happy to answer any questions you may have.

To see the latest updates on the radio show hosted by Gia, you can join the group on Facebook. The group is found right at www.facebook.com/groups/dawnofsh

www.ingramcontent.com/pod-product-compliance
Lightning Source LLC
Chambersburg PA
CBHW070804290526
45795CB00002B/616

* 9 7 8 1 4 9 3 7 3 6 4 4 7 *